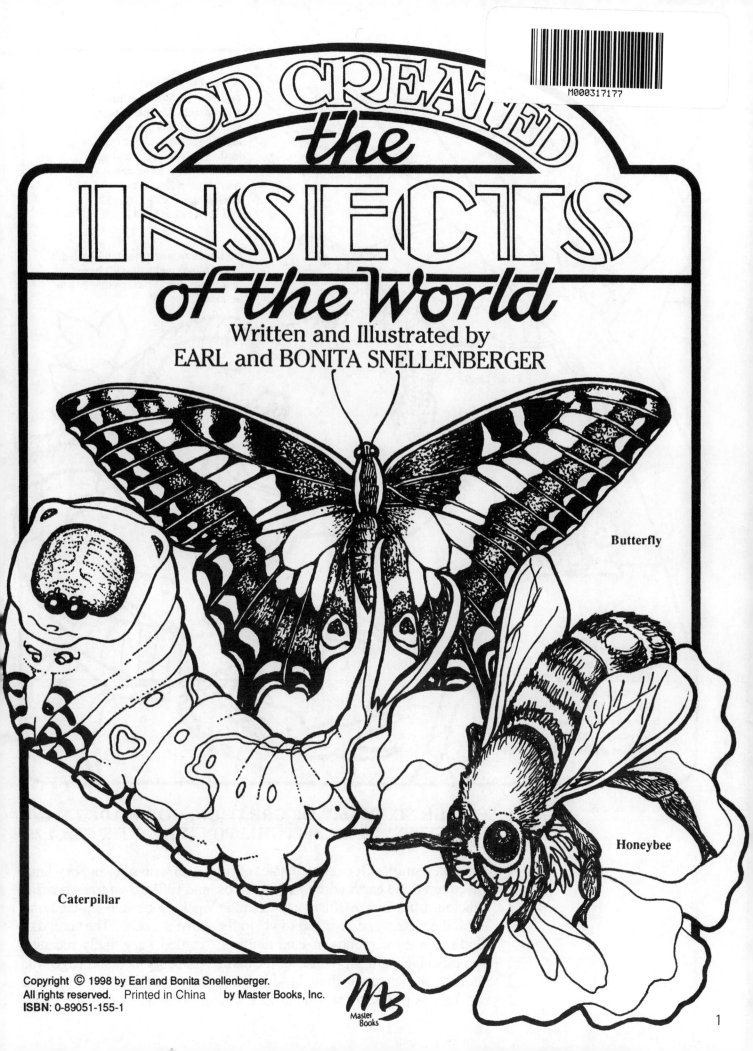

GOD CREATED the INSECTS of the World

Written and Illustrated by
EARL and BONITA SNELLENBERGER

Butterfly

Honeybee

Caterpillar

ISBN: 0-89051-155-1

Master Books

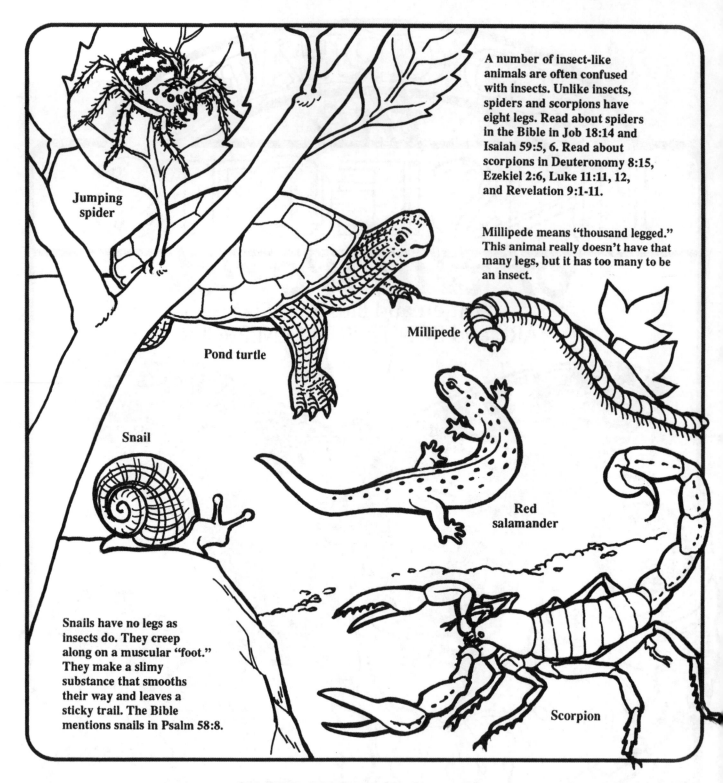

Jumping spider

Pond turtle

Snail

Millipede

Red salamander

Scorpion

A number of insect-like animals are often confused with insects. Unlike insects, spiders and scorpions have eight legs. Read about spiders in the Bible in Job 18:14 and Isaiah 59:5, 6. Read about scorpions in Deuteronomy 8:15, Ezekiel 2:6, Luke 11:11, 12, and Revelation 9:1-11.

Millipede means "thousand legged." This animal really doesn't have that many legs, but it has too many to be an insect.

Snails have no legs as insects do. They creep along on a muscular "foot." They make a slimy substance that smooths their way and leaves a sticky trail. The Bible mentions snails in Psalm 58:8.

ON THE SIXTH DAY OF CREATION, GOD MADE LIVING CREATURES "THAT CREEPETH UPON THE EARTH" (Gen. 1:25).

In the beginning, God created a beautiful world with seas and dry land. He covered the earth with grasses, herbs, and full-grown trees bearing delicious fruit. On the fifth day of Creation Week, God made sea-creatures to fill the waters and "winged fowl" to fly above the earth. The sixth day, God made three groups of land animals: "cattle," very likely meaning domesticable animals; "beasts of the earth," probably meaning large wild animals; and "creeping thing" — likely referring to all living creatures that crawl or creep close to the ground. Everything God made was "very good."

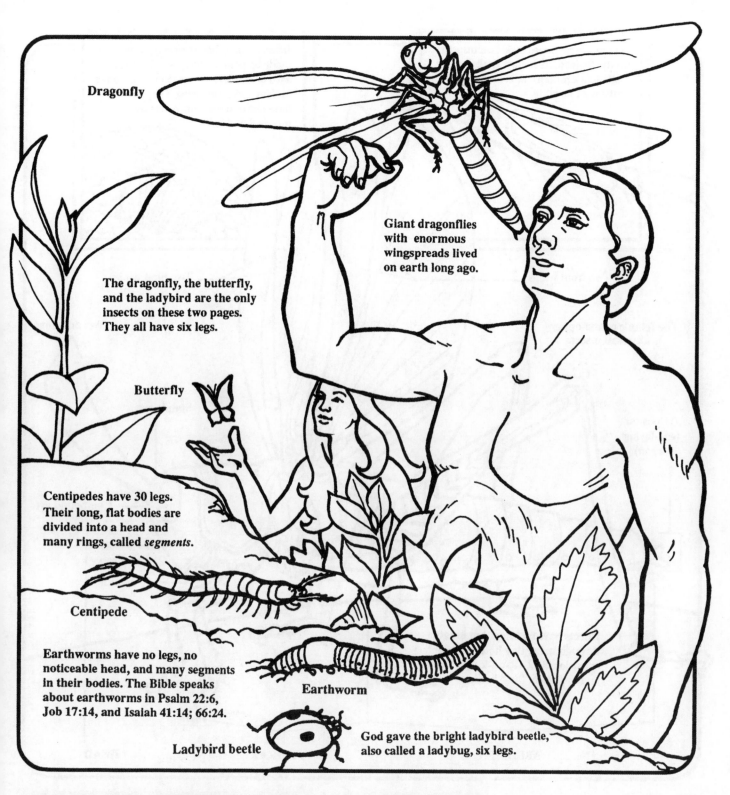

Dragonfly

Giant dragonflies with enormous wingspreads lived on earth long ago.

The dragonfly, the butterfly, and the ladybird are the only insects on these two pages. They all have six legs.

Butterfly

Centipedes have 30 legs. Their long, flat bodies are divided into a head and many rings, called *segments*.

Centipede

Earthworms have no legs, no noticeable head, and many segments in their bodies. The Bible speaks about earthworms in Psalm 22:6, Job 17:14, and Isaiah 41:14; 66:24.

Earthworm

Ladybird beetle

God gave the bright ladybird beetle, also called a ladybug, six legs.

SOME OF THE "CREEPING THINGS" GOD MADE IN THE BEGINNING ARE CREATURES KNOWN AS INSECTS TODAY.

God created creeping things with four legs, such as turtles and salamanders. God also made creatures that crawl on eight legs like spiders and scorpions. He made creatures that creep on many legs, such as centipedes and millipedes. But more than any other kind of creature, God created creeping things with *six legs*. God also created Adam and Eve, the first man and woman, on the sixth day. We do not know what Adam and Eve might have called creeping things with six legs in the beginning, but today all six-legged creatures are known as *insects*.

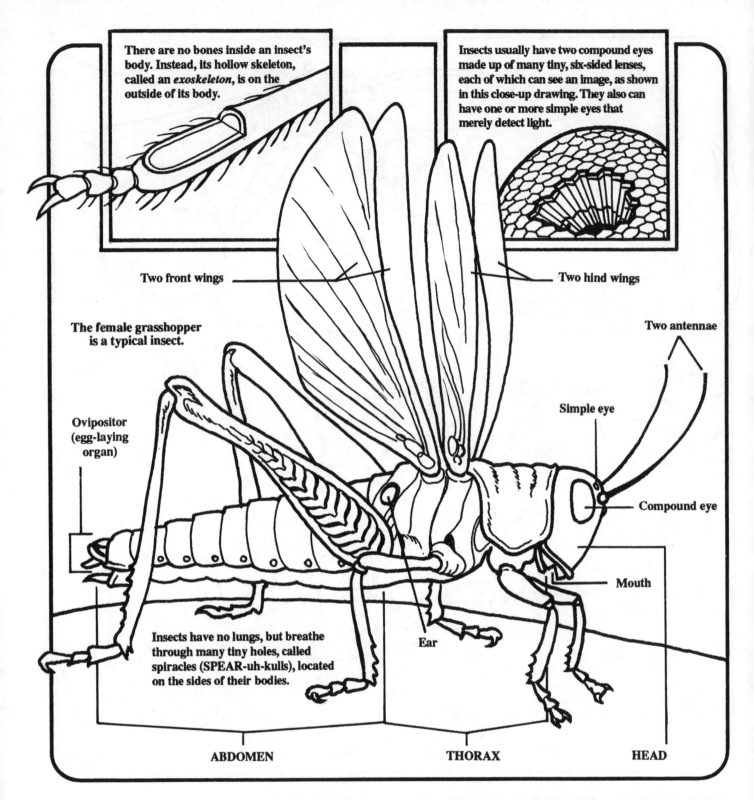

There are no bones inside an insect's body. Instead, its hollow skeleton, called an *exoskeleton*, is on the outside of its body.

Insects usually have two compound eyes made up of many tiny, six-sided lenses, each of which can see an image, as shown in this close-up drawing. They also can have one or more simple eyes that merely detect light.

Two front wings

Two hind wings

The female grasshopper is a typical insect.

Two antennae

Simple eye

Ovipositor (egg-laying organ)

Compound eye

Mouth

Ear

Insects have no lungs, but breathe through many tiny holes, called spiracles (SPEAR-uh-kulls), located on the sides of their bodies.

ABDOMEN

THORAX

HEAD

GOD MADE MANY DIFFERENT AND INTERESTING KINDS OF INSECTS, BUT ALL OF THEM ARE ALIKE IN SOME WAYS.

There are more than a million different types of insects on earth today, more than any other kind of animal life. The word insect means "in sections." All insects have a body divided into three main sections — the *head*, the *thorax* (THORE-ax), and the *abdomen* (AB-doe-mun). The hard, protective covering on the outside of their bodies is made of chitin (KITE-in), a material much like your fingernails. Insects also have two antennae on their heads, and six legs (three pairs) attached to the thorax. Of all creeping things, only insects have wings — most have four, some have two, and a few have none.

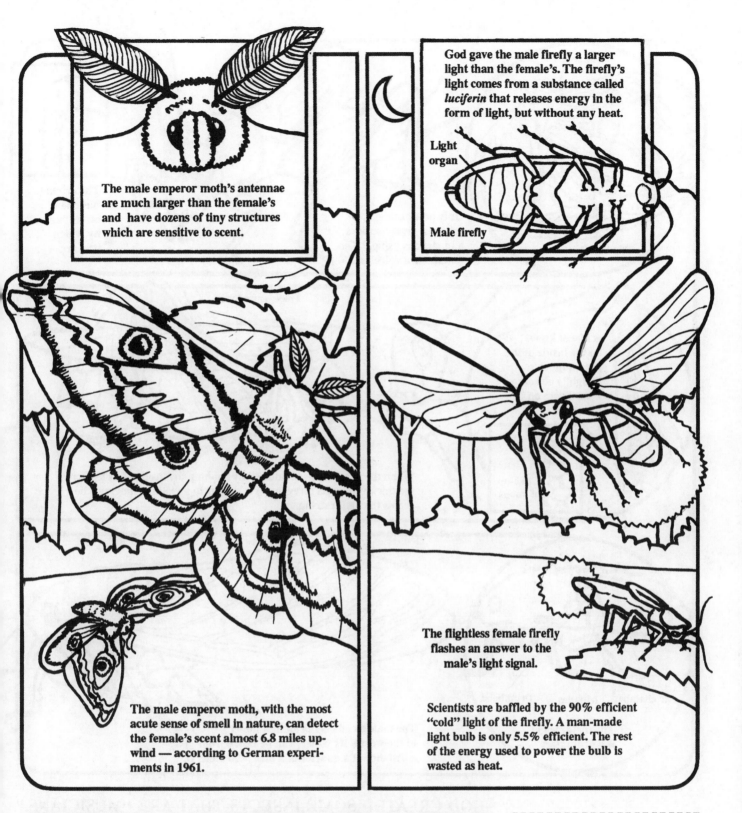

The male emperor moth's antennae are much larger than the female's and have dozens of tiny structures which are sensitive to scent.

God gave the male firefly a larger light than the female's. The firefly's light comes from a substance called *luciferin* that releases energy in the form of light, but without any heat.

Light organ

Male firefly

The male emperor moth, with the most acute sense of smell in nature, can detect the female's scent almost 6.8 miles up-wind — according to German experiments in 1961.

The flightless female firefly flashes an answer to the male's light signal.

Scientists are baffled by the 90% efficient "cold" light of the firefly. A man-made light bulb is only 5.5% efficient. The rest of the energy used to power the bulb is wasted as heat.

GOD CREATED A MALE AND FEMALE OF EACH INSECT; HE GAVE INSECTS DIFFERENT WAYS OF ATTRACTING A MATE.

God wanted each insect he created to be part of a pair, male and female. He gave insects special ways of attracting each other so they could become mates and have offspring like themselves. Emperor moths communicate by means of scent. The female moth exudes a special perfume, called a *pheromone*. The male moth can fly directly to her from several miles away by picking up the scent with its sensitive feathery antennae. Fireflies communicate with light signals. In the dark of night, male fireflies flash their flickering spots of light — which can be seen hundreds of yards away — to attract females.

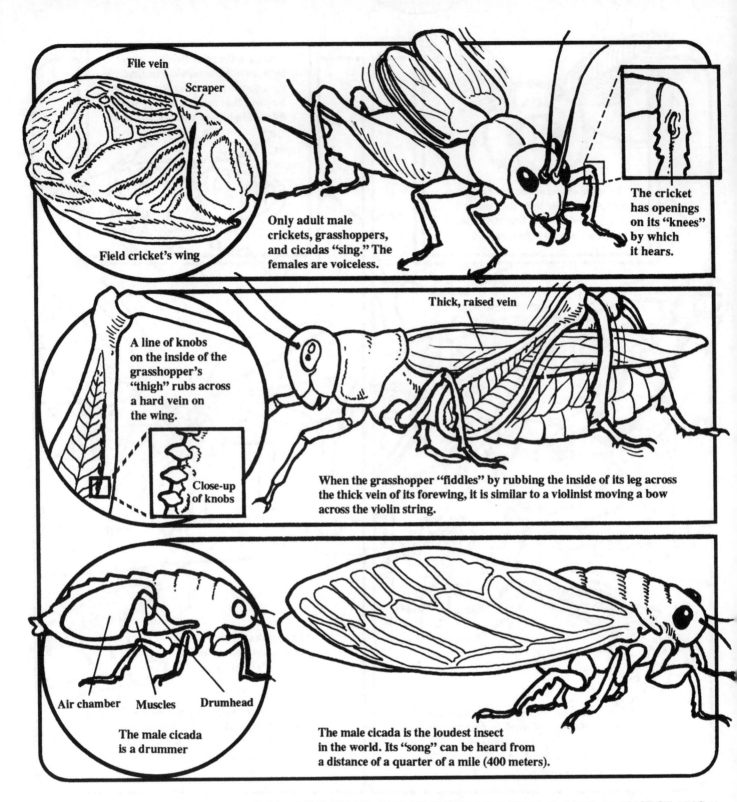

File vein

Scraper

Field cricket's wing

The cricket has openings on its "knees" by which it hears.

Only adult male crickets, grasshoppers, and cicadas "sing." The females are voiceless.

Thick, raised vein

A line of knobs on the inside of the grasshopper's "thigh" rubs across a hard vein on the wing.

Close-up of knobs

When the grasshopper "fiddles" by rubbing the inside of its leg across the thick vein of its forewing, it is similar to a violinist moving a bow across the violin string.

Air chamber   Muscles   Drumhead

The male cicada is a drummer

The male cicada is the loudest insect in the world. Its "song" can be heard from a distance of a quarter of a mile (400 meters).

GOD CREATED SOME INSECTS THAT ARE "MUSICIANS." THEY ATTRACT MATES WITH THEIR SPECIAL "SONGS."

The cheerful "fiddling" song of the field cricket is produced when the insect rubs its two wings together so the file-like vein on one wing moves against a sharp ridge, or scraper, on the other wing. The locust is a fiddler too, but its sound is made by rapidly raising and lowering its hind legs so knobs on their inner surfaces rub against rough, raised veins on their wings. God gave the cicada a large, hollow abdomen that acts like a drum. When tight muscles attached to a "drumhead" are released, the drumhead hits membranes that line the abdominal walls — producing the cicada's ringing music.

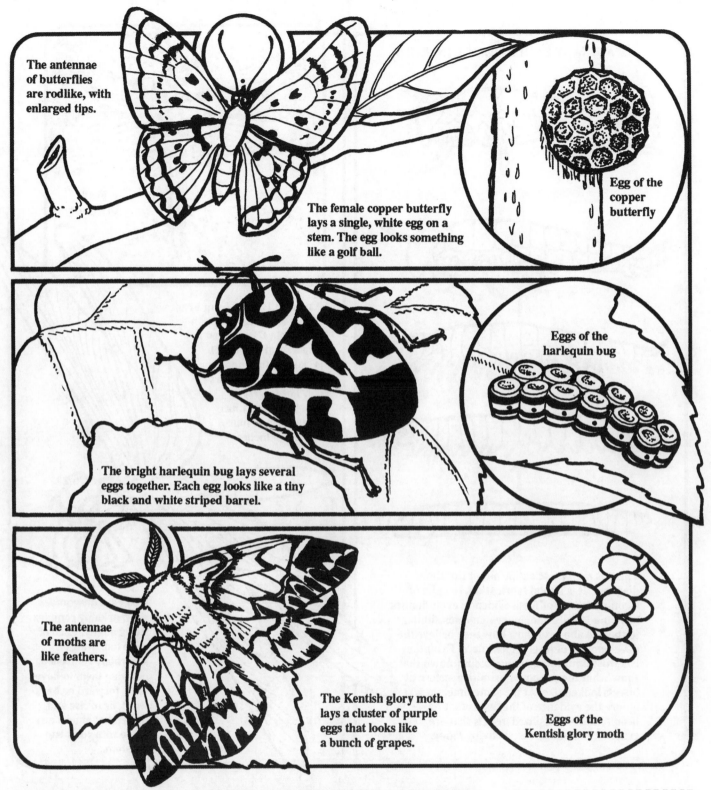

The antennae of butterflies are rodlike, with enlarged tips.

The female copper butterfly lays a single, white egg on a stem. The egg looks something like a golf ball.

Egg of the copper butterfly

The bright harlequin bug lays several eggs together. Each egg looks like a tiny black and white striped barrel.

Eggs of the harlequin bug

The antennae of moths are like feathers.

The Kentish glory moth lays a cluster of purple eggs that looks like a bunch of grapes.

Eggs of the Kentish glory moth

GOD PLANNED FOR INSECTS TO REPRODUCE BY LAYING EGGS THAT HATCH INTO YOUNG LIKE THEIR OWN KIND.

When the Bible tells us that each animal God created was "after his kind," it means God determined that any offspring of male and female mates will grow up to be just like them. To reproduce, most insects lay eggs, and the eggs of each kind of insect will **always** hatch into the **same** kind of insect. Each kind of insect's egg is unique; the egg's appearance and contents are unlike the egg of any other insect. God established this truth on the sixth day of creation: nothing but a grasshopper will ever hatch from a grasshopper egg. That is true for every kind of insect that God created.

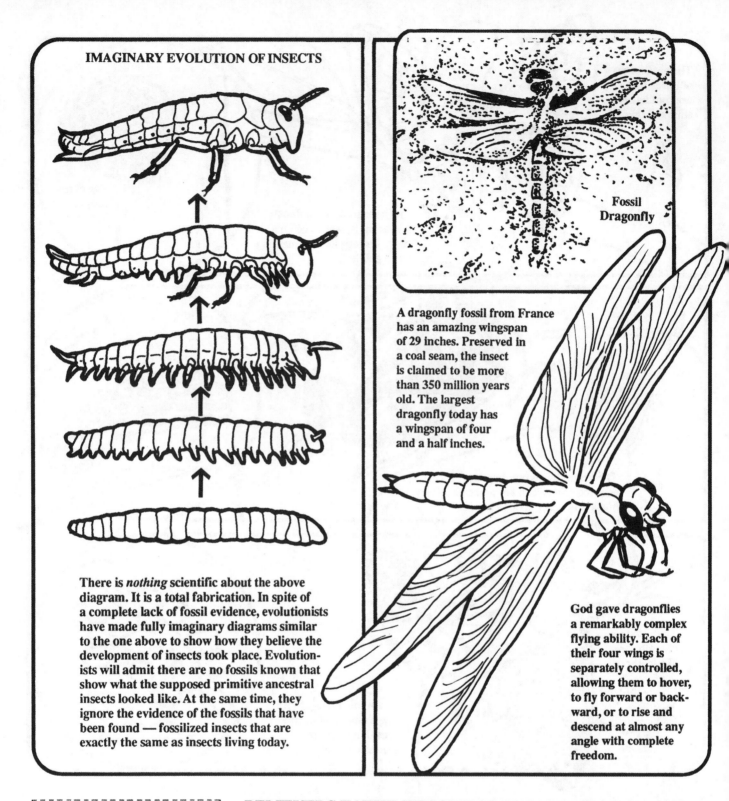

IMAGINARY EVOLUTION OF INSECTS

There is *nothing* scientific about the above diagram. It is a total fabrication. In spite of a complete lack of fossil evidence, evolutionists have made fully imaginary diagrams similar to the one above to show how they believe the development of insects took place. Evolutionists will admit there are no fossils known that show what the supposed primitive ancestral insects looked like. At the same time, they ignore the evidence of the fossils that have been found — fossilized insects that are exactly the same as insects living today.

Fossil Dragonfly

A dragonfly fossil from France has an amazing wingspan of 29 inches. Preserved in a coal seam, the insect is claimed to be more than 350 million years old. The largest dragonfly today has a wingspan of four and a half inches.

God gave dragonflies a remarkably complex flying ability. Each of their four wings is separately controlled, allowing them to hover, to fly forward or backward, or to rise and descend at almost any angle with complete freedom.

BELIEVERS IN THE THEORY OF EVOLUTION CLAIM THAT PRIMITIVE WORMS GRADUALLY CHANGED INTO INSECTS.

The Bible states the truth of God's creation, "For in six days the Lord made the heavens and the earth . . . and all that in them is" (Exodus 20:11) — and that includes insects! Yet, evolutionists foolishly claim that primitive, segmented worms developed into complex insects over tens of millions of years. In fact, the fossil remains of insects that evolutionists mistakenly claim to be millions of years old show that insects have **not** changed. For example, fossil dragonflies are not primitive at all. They are fully developed creatures — some larger than today's dragonflies, but the same.

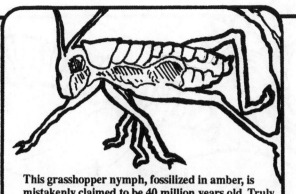

This grasshopper nymph, fossilized in amber, is mistakenly claimed to be 40 million years old. Truly only thousands of years old, it shows that grasshoppers always have grown by incomplete metamorphosis — just as God designed them to do when He made them on the sixth day of creation.

A few thousand years ago, probably before the great flood of Noah's day, a young grasshopper landed upon a coniferous or pine tree. Such trees produce a soft, gluey resin that oozes from cracks and wounds in their bark. When the grasshopper became mired in the resin, it was unable to escape the sticky trap and died — to become completely enveloped and perfectly preserved by the resin. In time, the resin hardened and was buried in the soil, possibly by the waters of the great flood. Finally, the golden fossilized resin, called *amber*, was unearthed on the shores of the Baltic Sea about 100 years ago.

A

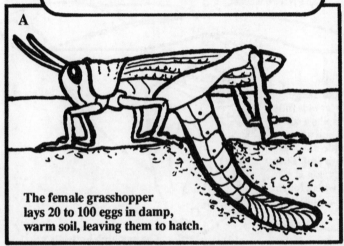

The female grasshopper lays 20 to 100 eggs in damp, warm soil, leaving them to hatch.

B

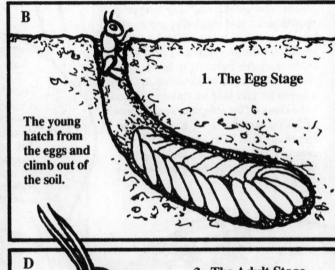

1. The Egg Stage

The young hatch from the eggs and climb out of the soil.

C

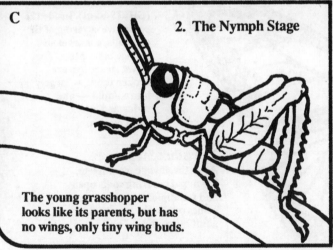

2. The Nymph Stage

The young grasshopper looks like its parents, but has no wings, only tiny wing buds.

D

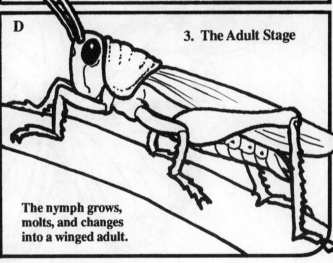

3. The Adult Stage

The nymph grows, molts, and changes into a winged adult.

A FOSSILIZED YOUNG GRASSHOPPER SHOWS THAT THE INSECT'S GROWTH PATTERN HAS ALWAYS BEEN THE SAME.

God planned for insects to grow in different ways. Some insects hatch from eggs as small-scale, exact replicas of their parents. They grow to adult size by *molting* — their old skin, or exoskeleton, splits when it becomes too tight, and they crawl out of it covered in a new, larger skin. Other insects, including the grasshopper, have a second growth stage between egg and adult. The grasshopper hatches out of the egg as a *nymph*, resembling an adult, but lacking wings. In a growth pattern called *incomplete metamorphosis*, the grasshopper molts to becomes a winged adult.

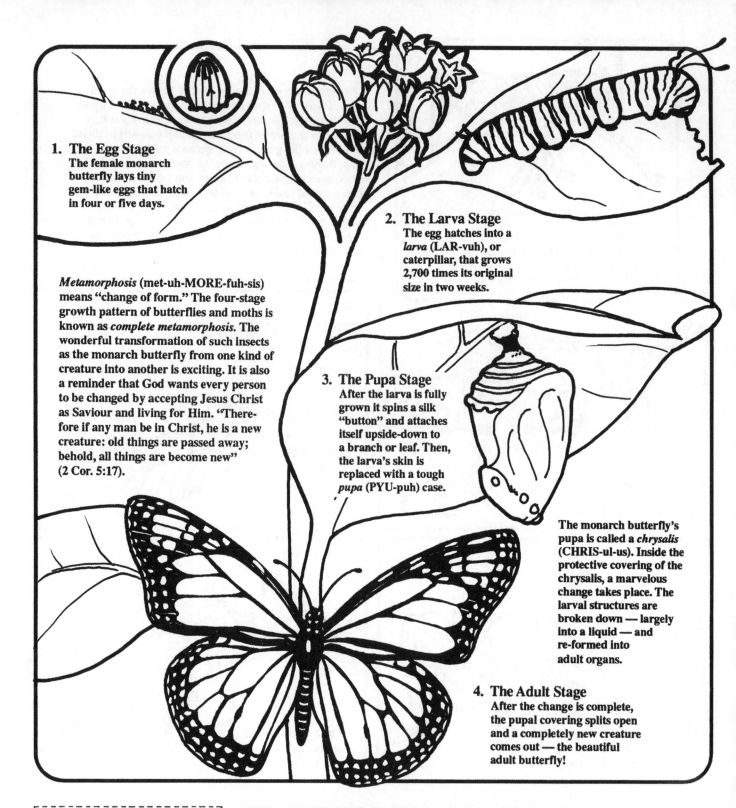

1. The Egg Stage
The female monarch butterfly lays tiny gem-like eggs that hatch in four or five days.

2. The Larva Stage
The egg hatches into a *larva* (LAR-vuh), or caterpillar, that grows 2,700 times its original size in two weeks.

Metamorphosis (met-uh-MORE-fuh-sis) means "change of form." The four-stage growth pattern of butterflies and moths is known as *complete metamorphosis*. The wonderful transformation of such insects as the monarch butterfly from one kind of creature into another is exciting. It is also a reminder that God wants every person to be changed by accepting Jesus Christ as Saviour and living for Him. "Therefore if any man be in Christ, he is a new creature: old things are passed away; behold, all things are become new" (2 Cor. 5:17).

3. The Pupa Stage
After the larva is fully grown it spins a silk "button" and attaches itself upside-down to a branch or leaf. Then, the larva's skin is replaced with a tough *pupa* (PYU-puh) case.

The monarch butterfly's pupa is called a *chrysalis* (CHRIS-ul-us). Inside the protective covering of the chrysalis, a marvelous change takes place. The larval structures are broken down — largely into a liquid — and re-formed into adult organs.

4. The Adult Stage
After the change is complete, the pupal covering splits open and a completely new creature comes out — the beautiful adult butterfly!

THE COMPLETE METAMORPHOSIS OF BUTTERFLIES IS MYSTIFYING EVIDENCE OF GOD'S AMAZING CREATION.

God planned for butterflies to grow in an incredible way. These beautiful flying insects lay eggs that hatch into young completely unlike themselves — crawling caterpillars! This baffles evolutionists, for these worm-like creatures never could have evolved into butterflies — because caterpillars don't lay eggs or reproduce at all! Instead, the caterpillar, or *larva*, which has a mouth for chewing leaves, eats, grows, and molts several times. Then the caterpillar changes into a *pupa*. The butterfly pupa is called a *chrysalis* with a hard shell for protection. In time, a liquid-nectar-sipping butterfly emerges from the chrysalis.

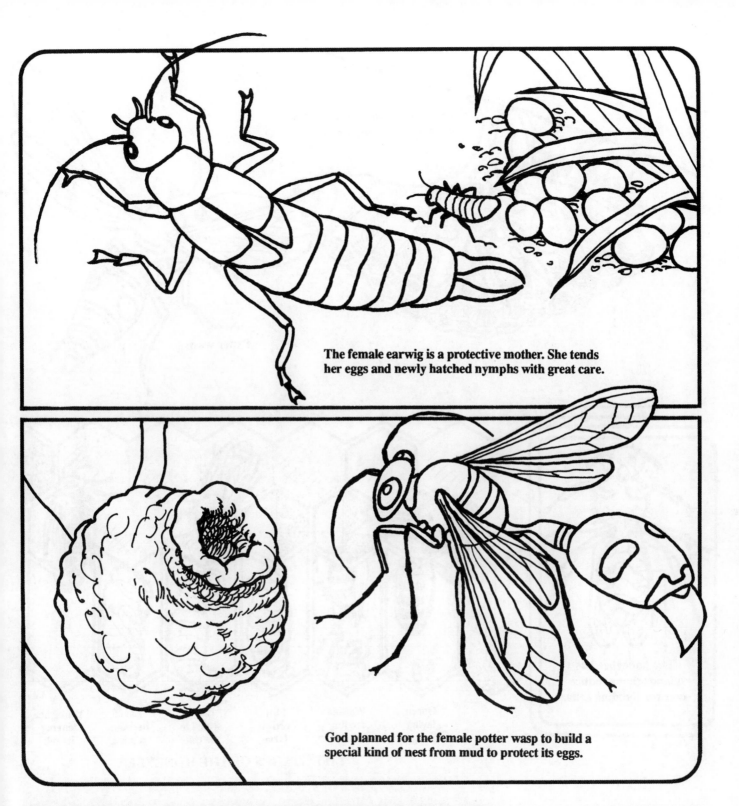

The female earwig is a protective mother. She tends her eggs and newly hatched nymphs with great care.

God planned for the female potter wasp to build a special kind of nest from mud to protect its eggs.

SOME INSECTS ARE VERY DEVOTED PARENTS, SOME ARE NOT. SOME INSECTS BUILD NESTS, SOME DO NOT.

The female earwig cares for her white, oval eggs almost like a mother hen —turning them and protecting them from harm. The earwig does not build a nest, but when the tiny nymphs hatch, she gathers them together beneath her body, feeding them until they are strong enough to care for themselves. Unlike the earwig, the potter wasp **does** build a nest. The female wasp finds a suitable branch and uses mud to fashion a nest that looks like a small clay jug. She lays her eggs inside it and collects food for the young to eat when they hatch. Then she leaves, never to see her offspring.

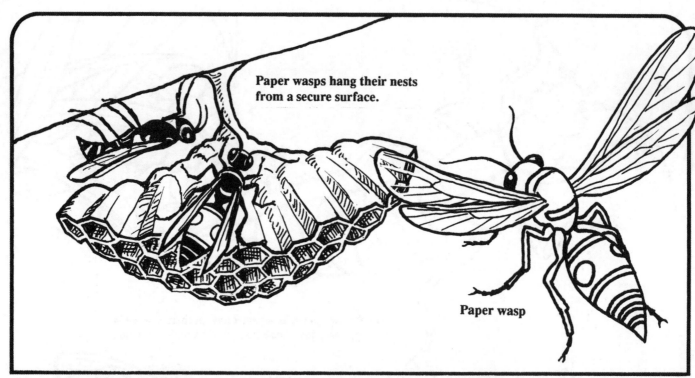

Paper wasps hang their nests from a secure surface.

Paper wasp

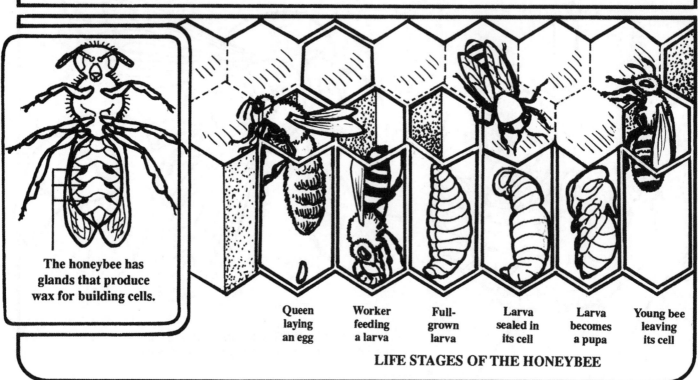

The honeybee has glands that produce wax for building cells.

| Queen laying an egg | Worker feeding a larva | Full-grown larva | Larva sealed in its cell | Larva becomes a pupa | Young bee leaving its cell |

LIFE STAGES OF THE HONEYBEE

SOME INSECTS WORK TOGETHER TO BUILD NESTS FOR THEIR YOUNG FROM VERY DIFFERENT MATERIALS.

Paper wasps build a nest of paper, made out of wood the wasps chew up with their strong jaws. An egg is placed in each of the nest's many cells. After hatching, the larvae stay in their cells and are fed until they pupate. Honeybees are *social insects*, living and working together in a *colony* of many thousands. God gave honeybees special glands that produce the wax they use to build their *hive*, a *honeycomb* — made up of six-sided cells. The colony's queen bee lays an egg in each cell, and the larvae are fed a mixture of pollen and honey, called *beebread*, by worker bees.

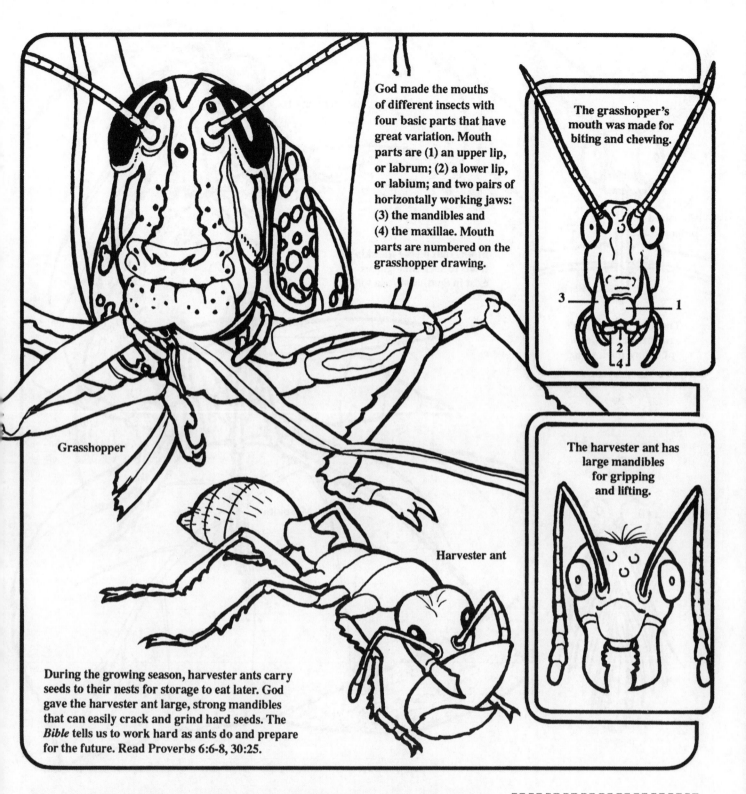

God made the mouths of different insects with four basic parts that have great variation. Mouth parts are (1) an upper lip, or labrum; (2) a lower lip, or labium; and two pairs of horizontally working jaws: (3) the mandibles and (4) the maxillae. Mouth parts are numbered on the grasshopper drawing.

The grasshopper's mouth was made for biting and chewing.

Grasshopper

The harvester ant has large mandibles for gripping and lifting.

Harvester ant

During the growing season, harvester ants carry seeds to their nests for storage to eat later. God gave the harvester ant large, strong mandibles that can easily crack and grind hard seeds. The *Bible* tells us to work hard as ants do and prepare for the future. Read Proverbs 6:6-8, 30:25.

ALL OF THE INSECTS GOD CREATED ATE PLANTS. HE GAVE INSECTS DIFFERENT KINDS OF MOUTHS TO EAT PLANT FOOD.

God had filled the earth with plant food for insects before He created them — trees loaded with ripe fruit, sap-filled stalks and stems, and tender green-leafed plants. God said, "To every thing that creepeth upon the earth, wherein there is life (that includes all insects), I have given every green herb for meat" (Gen. 1:30). To eat various kinds of plant food, God made insects' mouths with the same basic parts, yet wonderfully different. The grasshopper's mouth for chewing leaves is unlike the harvester ant's mouth — made for carrying seeds. Each insect's mouth is perfect in its own way.

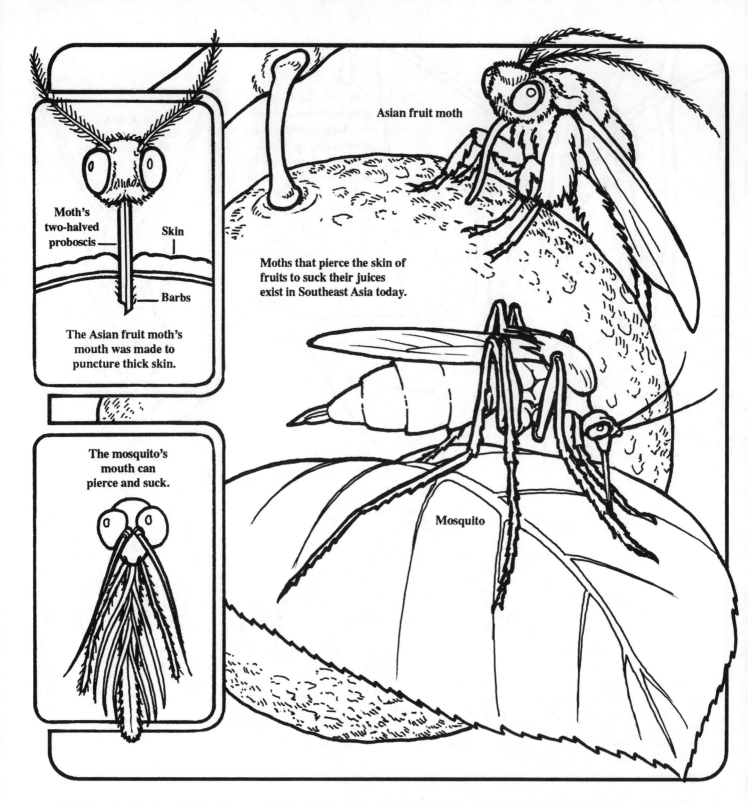

Asian fruit moth

Moth's two-halved proboscis

Skin

Barbs

The Asian fruit moth's mouth was made to puncture thick skin.

Moths that pierce the skin of fruits to suck their juices exist in Southeast Asia today.

The mosquito's mouth can pierce and suck.

Mosquito

GOD CREATED INSECTS WITH MOUTHS THAT CAN PIERCE FRUITS AND LEAVES LIKE HYPODERMIC NEEDLES.

God gave one moth mouth parts that even can go through the thick skin of oranges. The moth can rock its sharp, two-part proboscis from side-to-side until it pierces the fruit's skin to suck juice. Pressure from the juice causes tiny barbs on the proboscis to stand erect, anchoring the proboscis to prevent it from slipping out of the fruit. God gave the mosquito mouth parts that work like a hypodermic needle to pierce the surface of a leaf and suck out the liquids inside. In the beginning, some plants' juices must have had large amounts of hemoglobin — needed by the female mosquito in order to lay eggs that will hatch.

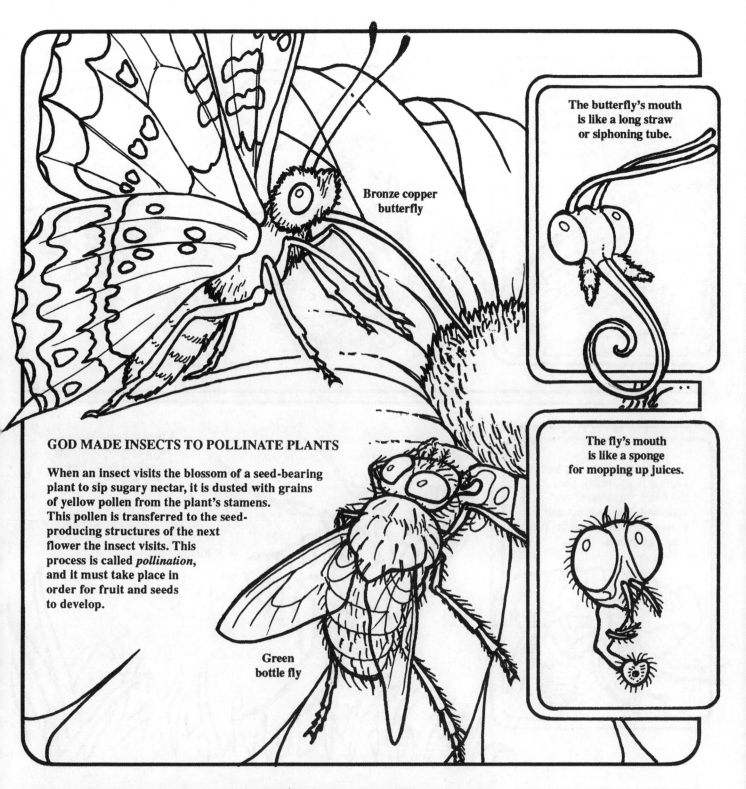

The butterfly's mouth is like a long straw or siphoning tube.

The fly's mouth is like a sponge for mopping up juices.

Bronze copper butterfly

Green bottle fly

GOD MADE INSECTS TO POLLINATE PLANTS

When an insect visits the blossom of a seed-bearing plant to sip sugary nectar, it is dusted with grains of yellow pollen from the plant's stamens. This pollen is transferred to the seed-producing structures of the next flower the insect visits. This process is called *pollination*, and it must take place in order for fruit and seeds to develop.

GOD CREATED SOME INSECTS WITH MOUTHS LIKE STRAWS AND OTHERS THAT HAVE MOUTHS LIKE SPONGES.

God made the mouth parts of most butterflies and moths like very long, flexible straws. They use them to suck sweet nectar from the centers of flowers. When they are not using their mouth parts, butterflies and moths can roll them up like a garden hose, out of the way. Perhaps God planned for the fly to feed on the half-eaten remains of fruits and vegetables left by other animals. God made the fly with the ability to spread powerful digestive juices on food that turn it to liquid. The broad tip of the fly's long mouth part is porous, and the fly uses it like a sponge to soak up liquids.

Delicate-looking butterfly wings have great structural strength — held together by rod-like veins like the supporting struts in an airplane wing.

Tortoise-shell butterflies

When the flea bends its legs to begin a jump, elastic pads in the flea's "shoulders" are squeezed. The pads act like springs to help launch the flea into high jumps.

A person could jump over a 50-story building if mankind could leap as well as a flea.

Flea

GOD MADE INSECTS THAT CAN FLY FAR ABOVE THE EARTH AND INSECTS THAT LIVE ON THE EARTH'S SURFACE.

The beautiful tortoise-shell butterfly may look fragile, but God made it far stronger than it appears. This remarkable butterfly is able to ascend high above the earth and fly over Mount Everest on a level with airplanes. In contrast, the tiny, wingless flea is an earthbound insect. But God made the flea the most amazing jumper in the world — leaping 13 inches in a single bound (33 centimeters) — which is 200 times the length of its body! The flea is little, but it has the ability to spring high up onto tall plants. God gave the flea a sucking mouth so it could live on plant juices.

ECTS *of the World*

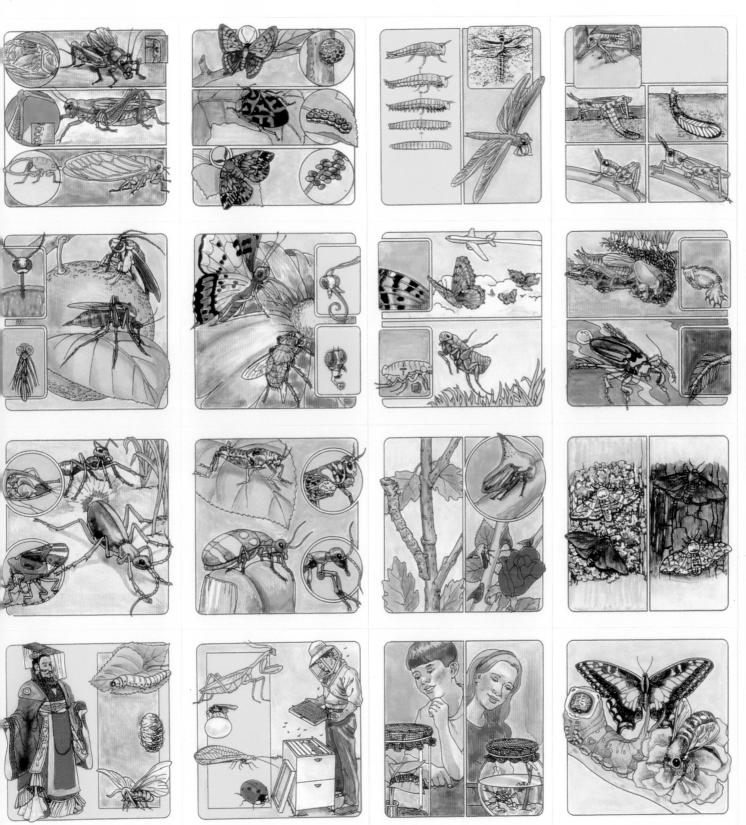

PLACE EACH STICKER BENEATH ITS MATCHING PICTURE. YOU MAY USE
THESE STICKERS AS GUIDES FOR COLORING THE PAGES OF THIS BOOK.

THESE 32 STICKERS SHOW THE INSECTS IN THEIR NATURAL COLORS
AS GOD MADE THEM. FIND THE MATCHING PICTURE FOR EACH STICKER.

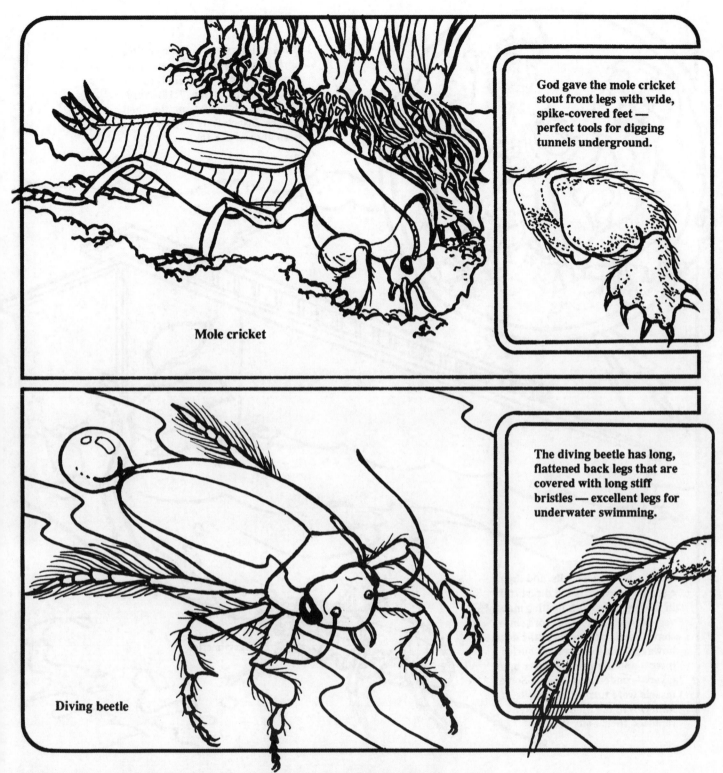

God gave the mole cricket stout front legs with wide, spike-covered feet — perfect tools for digging tunnels underground.

Mole cricket

The diving beetle has long, flattened back legs that are covered with long stiff bristles — excellent legs for underwater swimming.

Diving beetle

GOD MADE INSECTS THAT LIVE BELOW THE EARTH'S SURFACE AND OTHER INSECTS THAT LIVE UNDER WATER.

The mole cricket is perfectly suited for burrowing under the ground. God gave the mole cricket strong, flat front legs that serve as shovels for digging tunnels to reach the tender plant roots that are its food. The diving beetle was created to live successfully under water. God gave this insect long, flat hind legs that work like oars. To breathe under water, the beetle tows an air bubble that it has trapped between its body and wing cases. God designed each insect He created with bodies, wings, and legs that are exactly what it needs to live well — just where He decided to put it on earth.

Bible scholars are not in complete agreement that insects were among those creatures "wherein is the breathe of life" (Gen. 7:15) saved aboard Noah's ark from the flood waters. Insects may or may not have been aboard the ark.

Insects, lacking nostrils, and their eggs may have avoided destruction in the great flood on floating mats of vegetation. The fossil record shows some insects did perish in the deluge, however. The flood waters buried insects and plant life — layer upon layer — under tons of mud. Some insects were turned into fossils as minerals in the mud and water replaced their body tissues.

Tiger beetle

GOD'S WORLD WAS PERFECT FOR ALL LIVING THINGS, INCLUDING INSECTS, UNTIL ADAM AND EVE SINNED.

When Adam and Eve disobeyed God by eating the fruit of the tree of the knowledge of good and evil, sin entered the world. All of creation, insects included, suffered the results of sin — death and struggle. In time, the earth was so full of evil that the righteous Lord God decided to judge it with a global flood. But God is merciful, for He had Noah build an ark, and sent animals to the boat to be saved from the flood (Gen. 6:20). For those not aboard the ark, "all in whose *nostrils* was the breathe of life, of all that was in the dry land, died" (Gen. 7:22). Insects, of course, do not have nostrils.

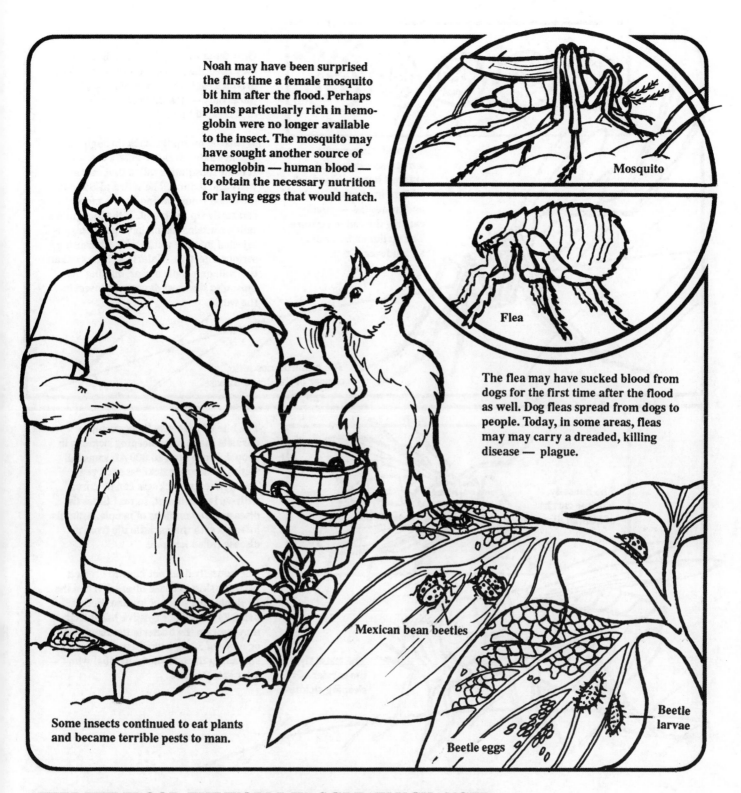

Noah may have been surprised the first time a female mosquito bit him after the flood. Perhaps plants particularly rich in hemoglobin were no longer available to the insect. The mosquito may have sought another source of hemoglobin — human blood — to obtain the necessary nutrition for laying eggs that would hatch.

Mosquito

Flea

The flea may have sucked blood from dogs for the first time after the flood as well. Dog fleas spread from dogs to people. Today, in some areas, fleas may may carry a dreaded, killing disease — plague.

Mexican bean beetles

Beetle larvae

Beetle eggs

Some insects continued to eat plants and became terrible pests to man.

AFTER THE FLOOD, THE WORLD WAS GREATLY CHANGED; SOME INSECTS NO LONGER COULD THRIVE EATING PLANTS.

The erosion of vital nutrients from the earth's topsoil by the flood must have been severe, and new plant life grown in depleted soil would have been deficient compared to its former nutrient-rich content. An extinction of many plants that were able to easily provide all the nutritional requirements of insects and other living things in the pre-flood world may have occurred as well. It is difficult, but not impossible, to live on a totally vegetarian diet today. It may have been even more difficult for Noah. Perhaps that is why God only permitted man to eat meat after the flood (Gen. 9:2).

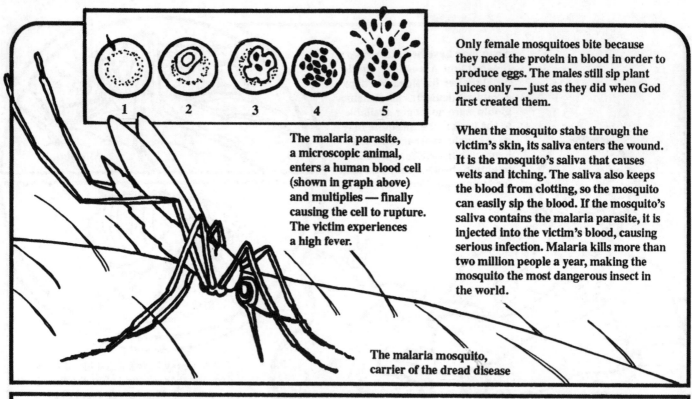

The malaria parasite, a microscopic animal, enters a human blood cell (shown in graph above) and multiplies — finally causing the cell to rupture. The victim experiences a high fever.

Only female mosquitoes bite because they need the protein in blood in order to produce eggs. The males still sip plant juices only — just as they did when God first created them.

When the mosquito stabs through the victim's skin, its saliva enters the wound. It is the mosquito's saliva that causes welts and itching. The saliva also keeps the blood from clotting, so the mosquito can easily sip the blood. If the mosquito's saliva contains the malaria parasite, it is injected into the victim's blood, causing serious infection. Malaria kills more than two million people a year, making the mosquito the most dangerous insect in the world.

The malaria mosquito, carrier of the dread disease

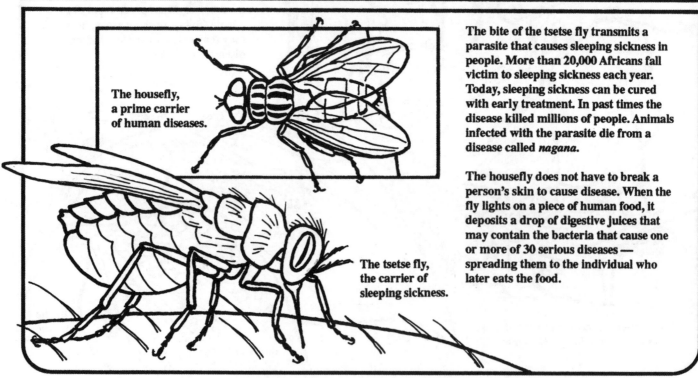

The housefly, a prime carrier of human diseases.

The tsetse fly, the carrier of sleeping sickness.

The bite of the tsetse fly transmits a parasite that causes sleeping sickness in people. More than 20,000 Africans fall victim to sleeping sickness each year. Today, sleeping sickness can be cured with early treatment. In past times the disease killed millions of people. Animals infected with the parasite die from a disease called *nagana*.

The housefly does not have to break a person's skin to cause disease. When the fly lights on a piece of human food, it deposits a drop of digestive juices that may contain the bacteria that cause one or more of 30 serious diseases — spreading them to the individual who later eats the food.

AS INSECTS' BEHAVIOR CHANGED DRASTICALLY AFTER THE FLOOD, THE RESULTS OF SIN TOOK A TERRIBLE TOLL.

In the beginning, everything that God created was "very good" (Gen. 1:31). Because of sin, God may have allowed beneficent processes and structures in nature to deteriorate to a harmful state in some cases. For today, such dangerous things as stingers, fangs, claws, poisons, germs, viruses, bacteria, and disease exist. The bites of certain kinds of mosquitoes carry such serious diseases as malaria, encephalitis, and yellow fever — resulting in the death of millions of people. Millons of others have died from sleeping sickness disease, spread by the blood-sucking bite of the tsetse fly.

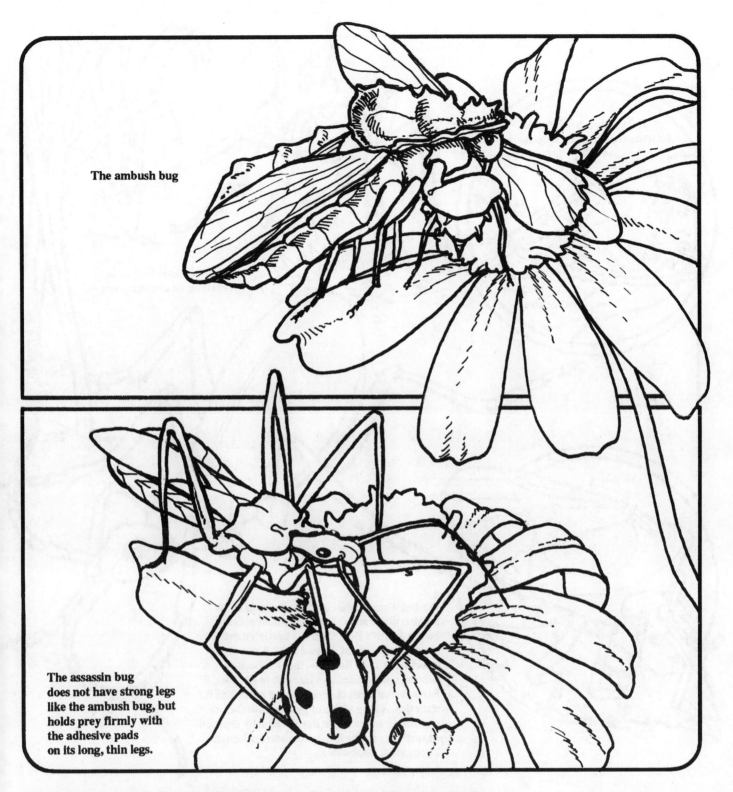

The ambush bug

The assassin bug
does not have strong legs
like the ambush bug, but
holds prey firmly with
the adhesive pads
on its long, thin legs.

SOME INSECTS TURNED FROM EATING PLANTS AND BECAME FIERCE PREDATORS, KILLING AND EATING OTHERS.

In some insects, structures once used to eat plants were now used in devouring their victims. In other insects, body structures may have changed — perhaps due to replacement as God caused previously recessive characteristics in their genetic code to became dominant. Predatory habits developed. Springing from its hiding place in blossoms, the ambush bug grasps its unsuspecting prey with strong front legs and tears it apart. In contrast, the assassin bug pumps a venomous saliva into a victim that reduces its tissues to a thick soup — then sucks the liquid from its hollow body.

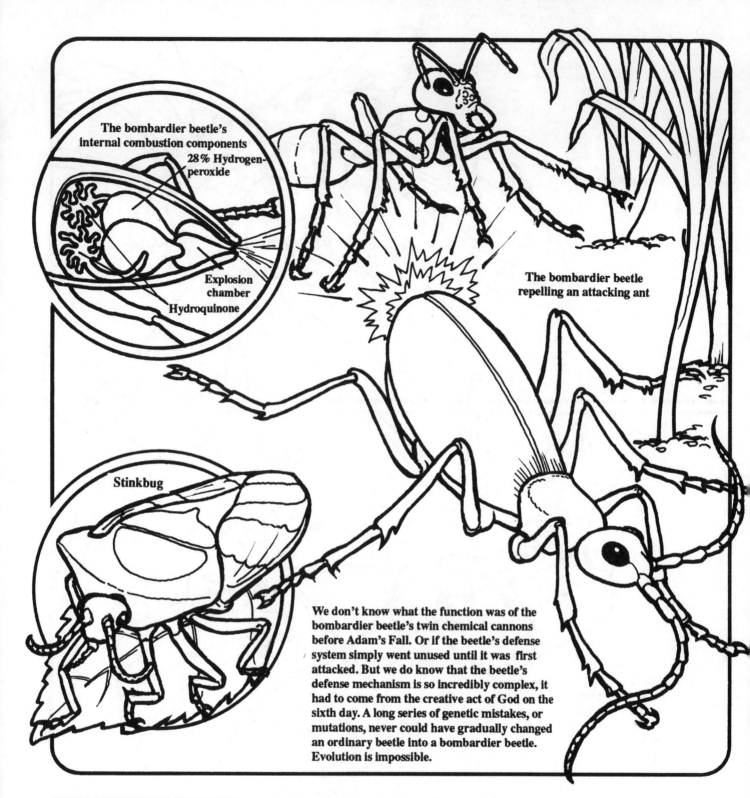

The bombardier beetle's internal combustion components
28% Hydrogen-peroxide

Explosion chamber

Hydroquinone

The bombardier beetle repelling an attacking ant

Stinkbug

We don't know what the function was of the bombardier beetle's twin chemical cannons before Adam's Fall. Or if the beetle's defense system simply went unused until it was first attacked. But we do know that the beetle's defense mechanism is so incredibly complex, it had to come from the creative act of God on the sixth day. A long series of genetic mistakes, or mutations, never could have gradually changed an ordinary beetle into a bombardier beetle. Evolution is impossible.

GOD KNEW SOME INSECTS WOULD BECOME PREDATORS; HE GAVE OTHER INSECTS AMAZING MEANS OF SELF-DEFENSE.

God knows the future and He made preparations for it. The Bible indicates that Adam's sinful rebellion — and thus the need for forgiveness of sin through the shed blood of God's Lamb, Jesus Christ — was known before the foundation of the world (Rev. 13:8; I Pet. 1:18-20). God knew animals would have to defend themselves in a fallen world, and He gave some insects remarkable chemical defense systems. When threatened, the bombardier beetle shoots a jet of boiling (212° F/100° C) chemicals at an attacker from twin combustion chambers. The stinkbug's foul smelling spray protects it.

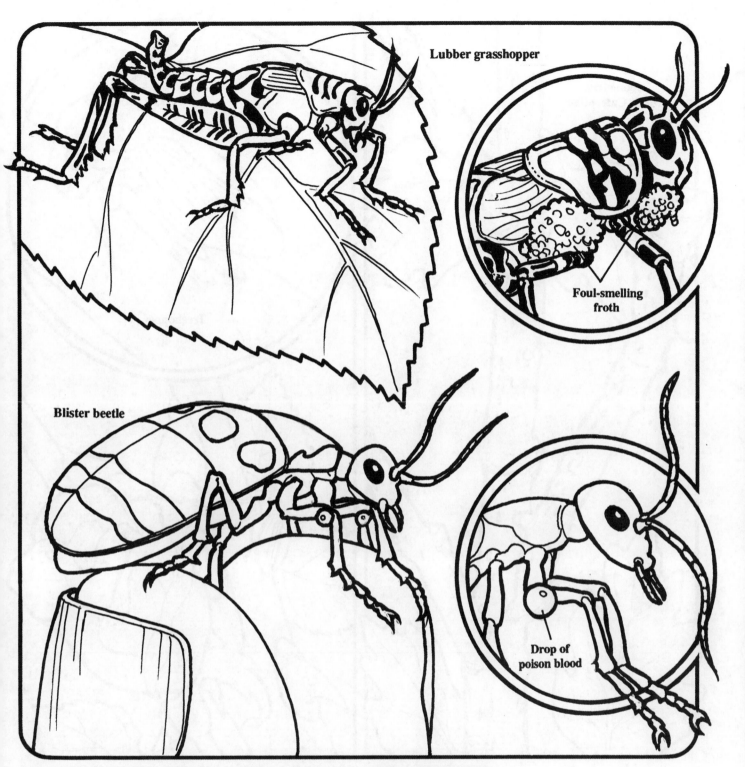

Lubber grasshopper

Foul-smelling froth

Blister beetle

Drop of poison blood

GOD GAVE SOME INSECTS ABILITIES TO ACTIVELY PROTECT THEMSELVES WITH HARMFUL CHEMICAL REPELLENTS.

The flightless lubber grasshopper is large and slow. However, God gave it the means to repel enemies. When disturbed, the lubber grasshopper oozes foul-smelling froth from its thorax and mouth with a loud hissing noise. The grasshopper bubbles air into a mixture of chemical poisons, phenol and quinones, that come from the plants it eats. The blister beetle has a different way of protecting itself called *reflex bleeding*. This beetle releases tiny drops of poisonous blood from joints in its legs that can cause blisters or welts on your skin — and can paralyze or kill small predators such as ants and spiders.

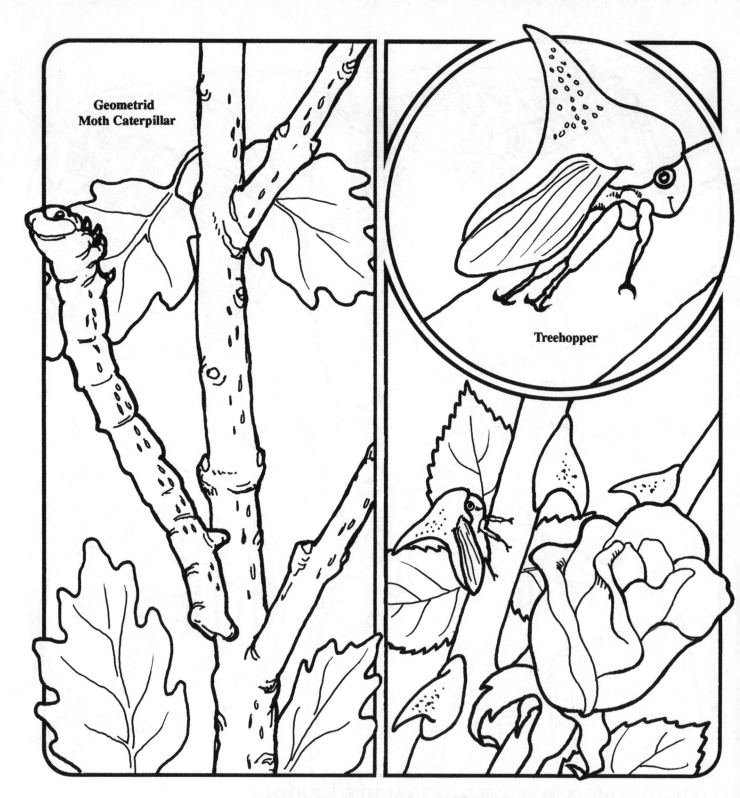

Geometrid Moth Caterpillar

Treehopper

SOME INSECTS ARE PROTECTED FROM PREDATORS BECAUSE GOD MADE THEM TO LOOK LIKE SOMETHING ELSE.

The geometrid moth caterpillar would make a tasty meal for a bird, but it is concealed in plain sight from predators. The caterpillar leans from a branch of the tree it eats and holds itself rigid to escape detection. Enemies mistake it for a twig. Treehoppers are small, winged insects that feed on plant juices. There are several different kinds, and God gave them curious and peculiar shapes. One treehopper appears to be just another thorn on the stem of a rose bush when it sits without moving. God also gave the treehopper strong legs so it can jump to safety if discovered. The Lord helps His creatures survive.

Dark peppered moths were easier for birds to see and capture *before* factory smokestacks of the Industrial Revolution blackened tree bark. There were fewer dark moths to lay eggs, so they were more rare.

Light peppered moths were easier for birds to see and capture *after* the Industrial Revolution darkened trees. In time, there were fewer light moths to lay eggs, so they became more scarce.

God gave many insects, such as the peppered moth, *camouflage* — protective coloration and pattern that make them appear to be part of the natural surroundings.

God wisely built variety into living things so they are better able to survive even as their surroundings change.

THE PEPPERED MOTH'S GOD-GIVEN CAMOUFLAGE HELPED IT SURVIVE AS ITS ENVIRONMENT CHANGED.

Before 1850, the peppered moth population of England was predominantly a pale variety — well-camouflaged against light, lichen-covered trees. However, when the smoke and soot of the Industrial Revolution began to coat trees with dark grime, the once rare dark variety of the moths began to flourish — for they were now less visible to bird predators. Evolutionary nature books and school texts deceptively use this as an example of "evolution in action." But this is not evolution — the change from one kind of life form into another — at all! Just as God planned, nothing but moth larvae will or can ever hatch from moth eggs.

Life Stages of the Fly

Eggs

Maggot

Pupa

Fly

Francisco Redi demonstrated scientifically that life can come only from life.

A SCIENTIFIC EXPERIMENT WITH FLIES SHOWED EVOLUTIONARY "SPONTANEOUS GENERATION" IS A FALSE BELIEF.

At one time people held a belief called "*spontaneous generation*," the idea that living things could spring to life on their own from non-living matter. After all, they saw that rotting meat, left out, was soon covered with maggots. However, spontaneous generation was discredited in 1668 when researcher Francisco Redi conducted an experiment. Placing pieces of raw meat in two jars, he covered one with a muslin screen and left the other open. In the open jar, flies laid eggs which hatched into maggots on the meat. No fly larvae appeared on the covered meat. Life can come only from life.

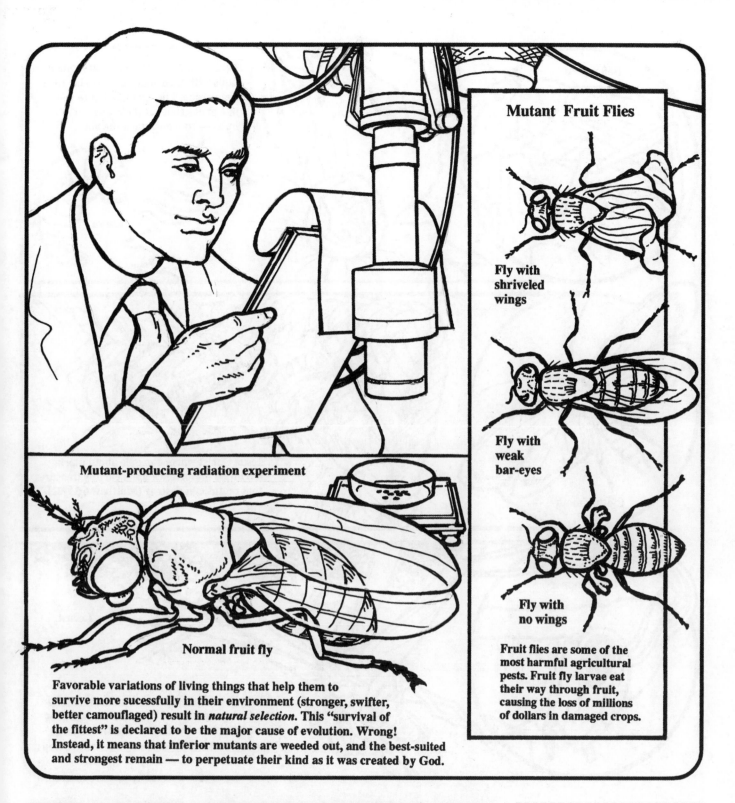

Mutant Fruit Flies

Fly with shriveled wings

Fly with weak bar-eyes

Fly with no wings

Fruit flies are some of the most harmful agricultural pests. Fruit fly larvae eat their way through fruit, causing the loss of millions of dollars in damaged crops.

Mutant-producing radiation experiment

Normal fruit fly

Favorable variations of living things that help them to survive more sucessfully in their environment (stronger, swifter, better camouflaged) result in *natural selection*. This "survival of the fittest" is declared to be the major cause of evolution. Wrong! Instead, it means that inferior mutants are weeded out, and the best-suited and strongest remain — to perpetuate their kind as it was created by God.

OTHER SCIENTIFIC EXPERIMENTS HAVE PROVED INSECT MUTATIONS DO NOT LEAD TO EVOLUTIONARY PROGRESS.

Mutation occurs when a living thing is altered or changed from its parental stock. According to evolutionary thinking, mutations over many, many generations leads to improvement from "primitive, lower forms" to "advanced, complex forms." Scientists subjected fruit flies, which produce new generations every 10 to 15 days, to mutant-producing experiments with chemicals and radiation for over 1,500 generations seeking evolutionary progress. There was none. Instead only damaged, distorted fruit flies hatched from eggs. The results demonstrated that mutations, rare in the first place, are 99.99% harmful or deadly.

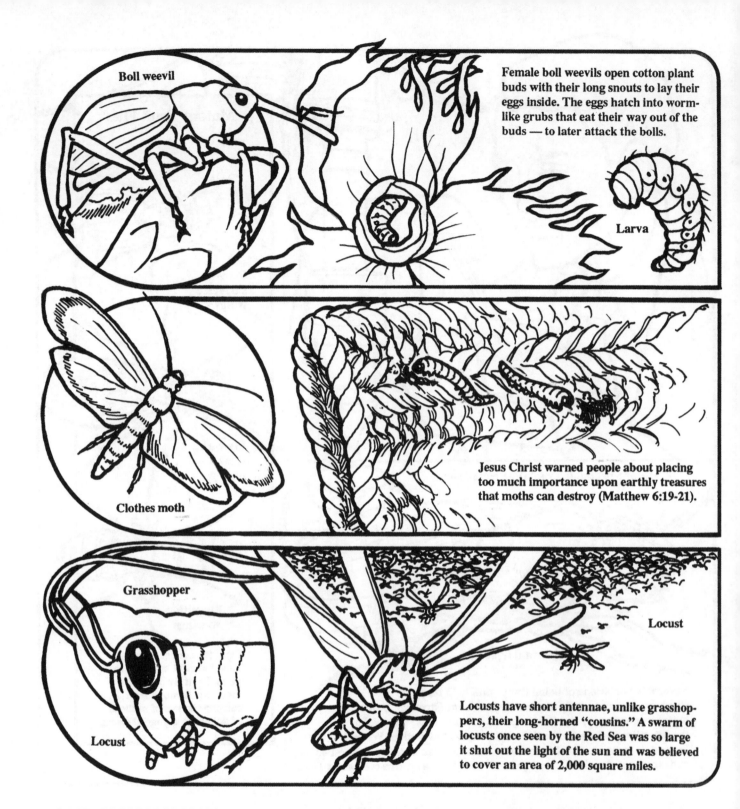

Female boll weevils open cotton plant buds with their long snouts to lay their eggs inside. The eggs hatch into worm-like grubs that eat their way out of the buds — to later attack the bolls.

Boll weevil

Larva

Jesus Christ warned people about placing too much importance upon earthly treasures that moths can destroy (Matthew 6:19-21).

Clothes moth

Grasshopper

Locust

Locust

Locusts have short antennae, unlike grasshoppers, their long-horned "cousins." A swarm of locusts once seen by the Red Sea was so large it shut out the light of the sun and was believed to cover an area of 2,000 square miles.

HARMFUL INSECTS HAVE CAUSED GREAT LOSS; SOMETIMES GOD HAS USED INSECT PLAGUES TO BRING JUDGMENT.

The boll weevil, a small beetle, feeds inside the *boll*s (seed pods) of cotton plants, causing multi-millions of dollars worth of damage to crops yearly. The clothes moth's larvae eat rugs, woolens, fur, leather, and hair — perhaps feeding for a year on prized possessions before they pupate. Since ancient times, great swarms of locusts have ruined crops — stripping fields of ripe grain completely bare of vegetation over vast areas. One of the ten plagues God brought against Egypt when the Hebrews were enslaved was the worst plague of locusts in history (Ex. 10:4-19).

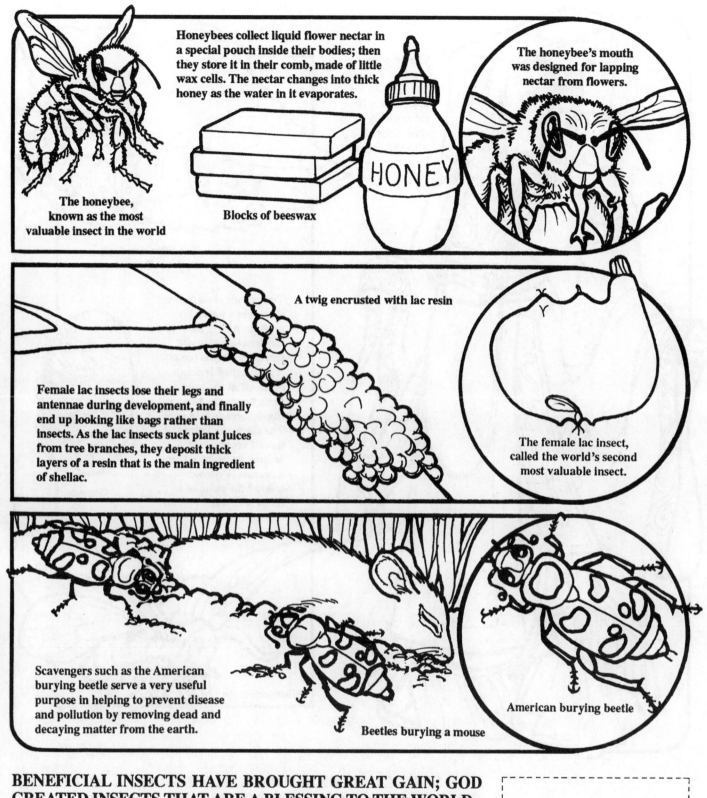

Honeybees collect liquid flower nectar in a special pouch inside their bodies; then they store it in their comb, made of little wax cells. The nectar changes into thick honey as the water in it evaporates.

The honeybee's mouth was designed for lapping nectar from flowers.

HONEY

The honeybee, known as the most valuable insect in the world

Blocks of beeswax

A twig encrusted with lac resin

Female lac insects lose their legs and antennae during development, and finally end up looking like bags rather than insects. As the lac insects suck plant juices from tree branches, they deposit thick layers of a resin that is the main ingredient of shellac.

The female lac insect, called the world's second most valuable insect.

Scavengers such as the American burying beetle serve a very useful purpose in helping to prevent disease and pollution by removing dead and decaying matter from the earth.

Beetles burying a mouse

American burying beetle

BENEFICIAL INSECTS HAVE BROUGHT GREAT GAIN; GOD CREATED INSECTS THAT ARE A BLESSING TO THE WORLD.

The only insect that produces food eaten by man, the honeybee is the source of valuable honey, used in cooking and as a sweet spread, and wax, used in making such products as candles and lipstick. The female lac insect secretes a resinous material that is used to make shellac, a major product of India that is widely used in varnishes, paints, stains, inks, and sealing wax. Burying beetles are important scavengers, removing decaying animal matter. They dig under the body of a small dead animal until it falls into the hole they have made. The animal's corpse serves as food for their larvae.

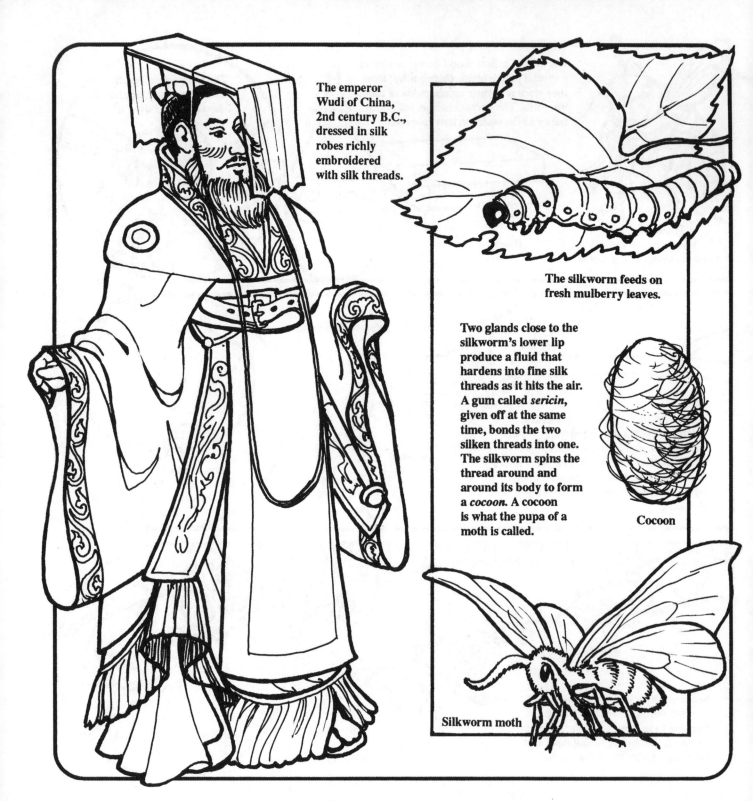

The emperor Wudi of China, 2nd century B.C., dressed in silk robes richly embroidered with silk threads.

The silkworm feeds on fresh mulberry leaves.

Two glands close to the silkworm's lower lip produce a fluid that hardens into fine silk threads as it hits the air. A gum called *sericin*, given off at the same time, bonds the two silken threads into one. The silkworm spins the thread around and around its body to form a *cocoon*. A cocoon is what the pupa of a moth is called.

Cocoon

Silkworm moth

THE SOURCE OF BEAUTIFUL SILK FABRIC — SHINY AND STRONG — IS AN INSECT, THE SILKWORM MOTH.

For over 4,000 years the Chinese have reared the silkworm moth, the insect that produces silk. Fed on a diet of mulberry leaves, the silkworm, the moth's caterpillar, spins its cocoon from a single thread extruded from salivary glands. The cocoon is soaked in hot water to soften it so the thread, up to 3,900 feet long and stronger than the same size thread of steel, can be unwound and woven into fabric. The production of silk remained a secret of the Chinese for more than 2,000 years. Once reserved for royalty, luxurious silk fabric is now widely available to everyone.

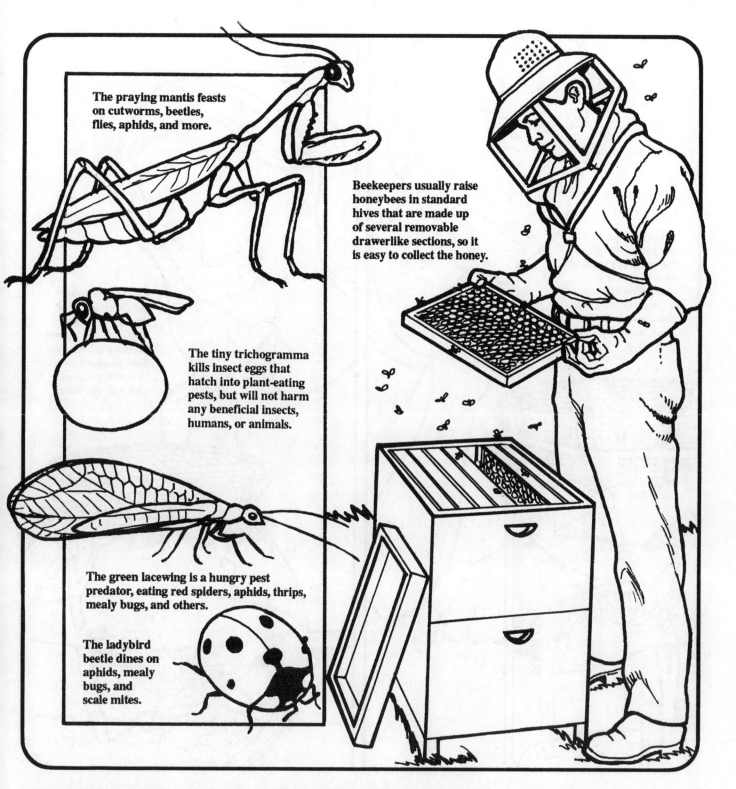

The praying mantis feasts on cutworms, beetles, flies, aphids, and more.

Beekeepers usually raise honeybees in standard hives that are made up of several removable drawerlike sections, so it is easy to collect the honey.

The tiny trichogramma kills insect eggs that hatch into plant-eating pests, but will not harm any beneficial insects, humans, or animals.

The green lacewing is a hungry pest predator, eating red spiders, aphids, thrips, mealy bugs, and others.

The ladybird beetle dines on aphids, mealy bugs, and scale mites.

BENEFICIAL INSECTS ARE A BLESSING FROM GOD, AND THEY CAN BE A GREAT HELP TO US IN OUR GARDENS.

There are several insects that are helpful in controlling destructive pests in flower and vegetable gardens: praying mantises, trichogrammas, green lacewings, and ladybugs. It is possible to order these beneficial insects through seed and garden supply companies. Many people enjoy beekeeping as an interesting family hobby, for honeybees are easy to handle and can be kept in both city and farm communities. Beehives are placed near gardens and fields, making it convenient for the bees to pollinate crops as they go from blossom to blossom. Their honey may be eaten or sold.

31

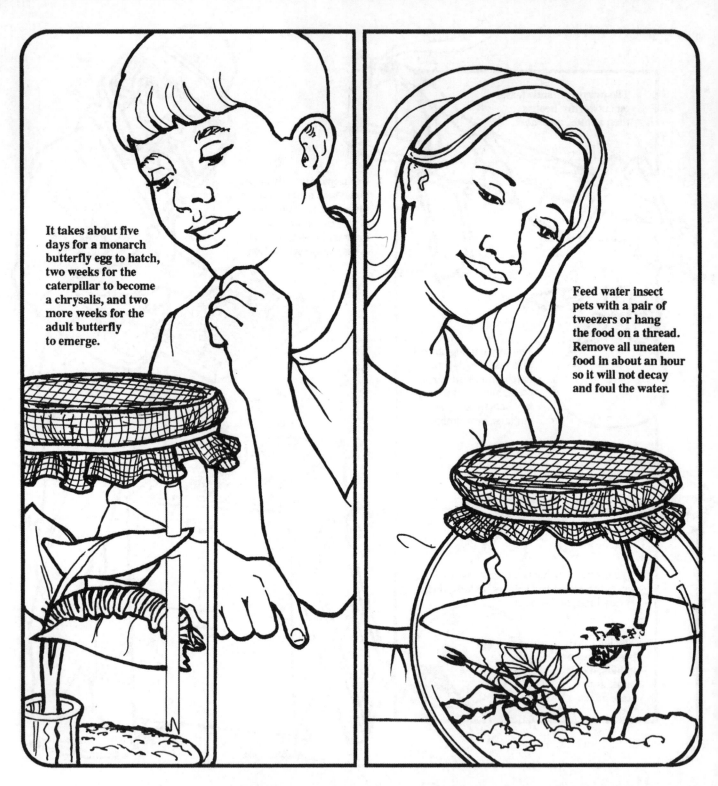

It takes about five days for a monarch butterfly egg to hatch, two weeks for the caterpillar to become a chrysalis, and two more weeks for the adult butterfly to emerge.

Feed water insect pets with a pair of tweezers or hang the food on a thread. Remove all uneaten food in about an hour so it will not decay and foul the water.

THERE ARE MANY INTERESTING ACTIVITIES YOU CAN ENJOY TO LEARN MORE ABOUT GOD'S AMAZING INSECTS.

Find monarch butterfly eggs on milkweed plants and keep them in a mesh-covered jar to watch the the insects go through their life stages. Keep plenty of fresh milkweed leaves for the larvae to eat. A half-filled bowl makes a home for water insects. Feed them bits of liver or fish. Collecting insects in display boxes will help you learn to identify them; a magnifying glass will show you things too small to see without a lens. Ant farms are an entertaining way of watching the daily life of these small creatures. And collecting fireflies to have a "living lantern" for an evening is enlightening fun!